Money Talks Bullshit Walks

The Entrepreneur's Guide to Productivity and Making More Money By Eliminating Distractions, Time Thieves and People Who Are Full of Shit

Omar Johnson

Copyright 2013 by Omar Johnson. Published by Make Profits Easy LLC

Profitsdaily123@aol.com

facebook.com/MakeProfitsEasy

Table of Contents

Introduction 5
    The time equals money fallacy 6
    Value your time 10
Chapter 1 – How Much Money do You Want? 12
    Determining value – pt. 1 13
    Productivity 16
    Determining you value – pt. 2 22
Chapter 2 – Time Thieves 24
    How do you defeat time thieves? 28
Chapter 3 – Interruptions 32
    How to avoid interruptions 35
Chapter 4 – Procrastination 43
    How can you avoid procrastinating? 45
Chapter 5 - Time Management 47
Chapter 6 – Information Overload 52
Chapter 7 – Delegate 57
Chapter 8 – People Who Are Full of Shit 60
Conclusion 65

Introduction

If there's one thing that you learn in business, it's that there are plenty of people who are so full of shit that you just want to scream. We see them every day, no matter where you go or what you're doing … they're out there stalking you, waiting for their chance –their opportunity- to pounce.

Entrepreneurship is the way that you take all of your knowledge, skills, talents, determination, bind it all together in the magic facet known as time, and through that you make money. That's what it's all about. When you can pull all of that together, you become successful.

The problem for many entrepreneurs is that even though you know that they're out there, you let them in. But the thing is … they're just more distractions that take us away from what's truly important, which is the business. So this book was written to try and help you recognize these thieves who look to steal the most precious thing from you …

… your *time*.

The time equals money fallacy

I'm going to operate on the assumption that you already know plenty about the phrase: time is money. You've probably heard about it from just about everyone in your life at some time or another.

We're taught about it in school. We're taught it by our parents who instilled the entire concept into our brains. We were made to believe in it and to focus our lives *on* it.

But it's wrong. Like so many things that you were taught in life, it's wrong. Time *doesn't* equal money. While you've been made to believe that if you're wasting time, you're not earning money and that's what it's all about, what do these two things have in common?

After all, let's just talk about it in terms of basic mathematics for a moment, shall we?

Time equals money.

Time = money.

That's like writing down A = B.

It doesn't imply that the two are the same … it states that they are.

So let's break this down a little bit more and try to make sense of what we're talking about here. If you have $5 in your pocket right now, what do you think that could buy you? It might be able to purchase a sandwich from a deli, a newspaper and bottle of Coke, or even a scratch off lottery ticket.

What do you do when you reach into your pocket and realize that it's not there anymore? Do you panic? Do you look around you and say, "Oh no, I've lost $5. I'm never, *ever* going to be able to replace it!"

No of course not. Sure, you may be upset that you lost the money, but it's just a minor inconvenience. You can earn it back. You can ***get money back***.

Now, let's talk about *time.*

Yesterday you had an argument with a friend, maybe a spouse, your child, or even your business partner. You didn't mean the things you said; you were upset and angry and he or she was really pushing your buttons and you felt that the best thing to do would be to 'get even.' Level the playing field, so to speak.

After you had some time to 'cool off,' you thought about what you said and wanted to take it back, but you can't. It was said, it's out there, and there's nothing that you can do to change that.

Just like that time when you were 15 and wanted to ask that cute girl to the dance, but you just couldn't find the courage. You look back on those days now and think how easy it should have been, but you didn't do it.

Now, can you go back to either of those moments and do them again? What about that day when you had so much work to get done, but you hardly did anything, choosing instead to read the news, watch some highlight reels from the sporting events the night before, or catching up on some of your favorite TV shows that you'd recorded. Now the deadline is upon you and you don't have enough time to get it done. Can you get that time back?

Of course not. You now have to live with the actions that you took (or didn't take) and that's the end of it. Sure, you can try and make amends, go beyond your deadline to deliver the goods, or regret the things that you didn't do, but you can't go back in time.

Not one single person in this world, in any era, has ever been able to go back in time.

Once the minute is *spent*, or lost, it's gone. There is no getting it back.

Now, does that sound like money? Does that appear to have anything resembling the same thing as money? Absolutely not. In truth, once you've spent or lost the minutes in your life, they are gone.

That's why time is so precious. You only have this moment to do something and then the moment will be gone, never to come back to you again. You can spend an hour trying to apologize for a wrong, make amends for being lazy, or not getting something done that you had every opportunity to do, but you can't get that time back.

Once time is gone, it's gone.

The same can't be said about money.

What happens if you make an investment and it doesn't work out? You lose that money. The more money you invested and lost, the more it's going to hurt you, but that doesn't mean you can't get it back, right? You can't go back and undo that investment, but you can learn from it and then go out and get that money back and try again.

Once the minutes of your life are gone, while you may be able to learn something from them, they're gone. There's no getting them back.

So time definitely *does not* equal money.

Value your time.

That's why it's crucial that you learn to begin to *value your time*. Time is the one thing that we all have in equal measure, no matter how rich or poor you are. Your time is as valuable to you (or should be) as it is to the person making billions of dollars a year.

Donald Trump gets the same 24 hours in a day as you do. So does Bill Gates and Warren Buffett. They value their time and are obviously quite productive into turning their time into money and that my friend is the essence of entrepreneurship. Converting your knowledge, expertise, talent and sheer will through investment of your time into money.

Now to really get filthy stinking rich like the aforementioned billionaires you will have to learn how to master and leverage the time of others and we will cover that a little later in the book when we discuss the topic of delegation.

To reiterate, in order to be successful as an entrepreneur, you absolutely must value time first and foremost. Once you begin to value your time in the proper way, you're going to want to protect it in the best way that you can and that means by being ruthless with anyone or anything that tries to steal away your time. When people or things steal away your time, they are stealing away from your productivity which is going to have an adverse impact on your bottom line. How much of an adverse impact that it has on your bottom line all depends on the amount of productive time you allow these nuisances to steal away from you. So a word to the wise don't let anyone or anything that is frivolous and unimportant steal your time and don't foolishly give away your time fruitlessly.

To stay on top or rise to the top as an entrepreneur you must always remember and embed it in your brain that TIME is a serious business. In fact turning TIME into money is your only business. So beware of all of the time thieves, countless distractions and the people who are full of shit because if you don't it will be the death of your business. To state it more poetically money talks, bullshit walks.

Chapter 1 – How Much Money do You Want?

What do you want to earn? Come on, you can share it … it's just between us. Just say a figure that you believe you're worth and how much you want to make on a regular basis.

Okay, let's be realistic here. While there's no reason why you shouldn't be able to make millions of dollars every year, we have to start somewhere and build from that, so let's keep the millionaires club on the backburner for a moment, shall we?

What's the real amount that you want to earn every year? For some, it might be $150,000 a year. For others it might be more, like $250,000 or even $500,000 per year. These amounts are of course all attainable goals for any entrepreneur. *If* they value their time, that is.

Every business is going to be different. If you're going to start a motivational speaking company, for example, and you're going to be the only employee –the one who will be not only marketing and booking engagements, but also the one who will be presenting your material to all of your clients, then you're going to be somewhat limited.

If, on the other hand, you're planning on training a dozen exceptional speakers to go around the country presenting *your* material to clients, then you could be looking at quite a bit more earnings potential. Even if you hire one employee who will answer phone calls and email inquiries and book dates for you to speak gives you more opportunity to earn what you're worth (your value).

However, in the beginning, you need to understand what you're true value is and be realistic about it.

Determining value – pt. 1

Let's talk about this a bit more, shall we? What is your value when it comes to your business venture? This could be what you want to earn, what you're going to charge per hour, or what you're going to charge for certain merchandise. You have bills to pay, maybe a lease, car payments, equipment, and perhaps stock. You have, in other words, expenses. Don't we all?

So at the very least, you're going to have to earn enough money to cover these basic expenses. Then, of course, you don't want to be working every day of your life just to break even. You want to *make money!* Yes … we want to make money. That's what the American Dream and entrepreneurship are all about, working hard to better your life, to get the things that you want and to enjoy life to the fullest.

So then you want to earn a certain amount of profit.

So go ahead. What do you need to earn to not only break even, but to make a profit. Now, you have your figure. Let's say, for argument's sake, that you want to earn $250,000 a year for the first couple of years. That will not only cover your expenses, but also your mortgage, vacation, and help you begin to build *real* wealth or invest it back into your business to expand it even more.

Awesome.

Next, you should have a pretty good idea about how many hours you plan on working throughout the week, each week, every week, throughout the year. Is it going to be 40? Or maybe you're going for 50 hours a week. Perhaps you're planning on dedicating 60 hours or more to your new business every week. As I said, every business is going to be different, so you should have a pretty good idea about how much you want to earn in the year and then have an idea about how many hours you'll need to work during the week to achieve that goal.

When you have good employees working for you, then you're going to find that it's easier to earn more while working a bit less, but in the beginning, more entrepreneurs tend to devote a lot of work to their efforts.

So let's divide your annual target earnings ($250,000) by 52 weeks per year. That gives us a total weekly earnings rate of $4,807 (and change, but we won't worry about the change … you can keep that in your piggy bank for a future vacation or your kid's college fund).

Now, if you plan on working for 50 hours per week, then you're going to need to earn $96 per hour in order to reach your goal.

Piece of cake, right?

You sure about that?

This is what most new entrepreneurs think when they make this calculation. So for the moment, figure out what your number is and we'll go with that. Right now, we'll use the $96 per hour as your guide.

Productivity

Now, are you *really* going to be working hard and being productive for 10 hours a day? You are? Seriously?

You mean there's not going to be any time taken away from you for work that you're actually going to get done for a client? Every hour that you devote to your business, all 10 of them, 5 days a week, all year long, is going to be directly working on something for a client? This is known as a billable hour.

You've probably heard the term 'billable hour' before because it's how lawyers charge for their service. However, you probably aren't going to be working on a billable hour structure, at least not right now. You're going to be working based on a *per project* structure. Whether you're creating documents for a client or consulting, you can only really charge for the hours that you'll be working on it.

So let's say that you have a project that you bid on for a client. You estimated that the project will take you 10 hours, so you charged $960 for the project. Not bad, right? You're going to hit your mark and everything's going to A-O-K.

So, be honest … are you really devoting 10 solid hours to that project? You mean that you're closing your door and shutting out all of those distractions?

What about the call from another client who wants to talk about something? What about this client who hired you for this job? What if he calls to talk to you more about it? Did you calculate that time into your estimate? What about the time that it took you to find this job, place a bid, and interview for it? Did you calculate those expenses into your figure?

You see, productivity is not what you think it is. While you may want to believe that you're going to be productive throughout your day (and you may work hard, never take a lunch break, and feel like you're constantly on the move, you're not being productive for all of that time). Depending on the type of work you do, you might have true productivity hovering between an hour a day to four hours. Few companies or businesspeople are more productive than that.

The misconception of productivity

This isn't an easy concept for a lot of people to grasp. We prefer to think about ourselves as being productive, as working hard, as doing the right thing. But this isn't about you not working hard, because you probably are; you probably drive your spouse crazy with your long hours and hard work that you put into your business.

But there are other things that take away from true productivity. Phone calls, people wanting your time, distractions. You might have to research some aspect for this new project, something that you didn't know about and you want to make sure that you understand it because if you don't, then you're not going to get it right and that won't go over too well with your new client.

Did you calculate that into your bid? Maybe, maybe not.

However, think hard about how productive you truly are on any given day. Looking back at all of the jobs that you've completed for clients during the past month, you may be pleased with the level of work and dedication that you showed. Now, calculate how many hours it took you to complete each one. If you haven't tracked this information before, then you might be surprised.

Take the number of hours that you're in your office working, how many hours it takes you to complete a project (actual time working on it), and then see how your productivity matches up.

Most people will be able to recognize the fact that even though it took you 10 full hours to do, you spent three days completing it. That would be thirty hours because you weren't working on any other projects for clients.

And that's about the average of true productivity, and it's what you should expect to be able to do on a regular basis.

Now, you may be wondering what you could have been doing the rest of the time since you only got that one job completed. The truth is, probably allowing yourself to be distracted, like most of us do.

Now, if you are productive for about one-third of your working day, then you need to recalculate what your hourly rate should be (what you should charge clients for your services). You may have wanted to earn $23 per hour, but your billable time should actually be $96 x 3, which would come out to $288 per hour.

You see, if you had bid $2,880 on that one project, then you would have achieved your target for those three days that you spent working on it.

But I wouldn't have gotten the job if I bid that much, you might be thinking. Maybe. Maybe not. You don't know that. Yes, for some people, money is an issue, but for others, it's about getting experience, creativity, professionalism … all of the characteristics that make someone successful.

When you begin to concern yourself with all of the residual issues that surround yourself and whether you're going to be hired or get the jobs you want, then you're missing the point. Yes, sometimes you're going to have to lower your expectations until you gain more experience or build a more impressive portfolio, but in the beginning, you need to be able to calculate how much you need to *charge* in order to earn your *value*.

If your competitors are charging less than you and have more experience, then you may have to sacrifice until you can prove to potential clients that you're worth the *value* that you're demanding. If your skills, knowledge, and experience can support your asking price, then you focus on that and don't look back.

Okay, so you now know that you're worth $288 per hour. You might never have thought about that before, but there it is. You're worth $288. Maybe you're worth $588 per hour. Maybe you're worth more.

It doesn't matter the number, as long as it is in line with your true *value*.

Next, let's talk about the distractions that erode our daily productivity.

A potential client calls and wants to discuss a project with you. They spend ten minutes on the phone going over some preliminary questions, then want to schedule an interview. Those ten minutes just cost you $288 divided by 6 (60 minutes in an hour, 10 minutes = 1/6), or $48.

Your wife who just walked into your office to talk about what color the living room should be painted or to ask you whether you paid the electric bill this month, took about 5 minutes of your time. This would be another $24.

Another phone call. A leaky faucet. A short break to sit back and relax. An employee who is having a problem with an assignment, and you take the time to mentor him or her.

Every single thing begins to attach a dollar amount to it and you begin to see just how costly those distractions can be.

When you work on projects for clients, you're not going to get your estimates right every time. Some clients are particular and demand more, which leads to you earning less. Some jobs will be easier, taking less time, which will earn you more. Somewhere you'll need to fine-tune that balancing point. For now, though, you should begin to figure out what your true value is.

Determining you value – pt. 2

So now that you have a basic understanding of value and productivity, and how the latter can and does affect the former, let's reevaluate your value.

If you still want to earn $250,000 per year, the base would be $96, considering you're productive for each of the 10 hours that you put into work every day.

We know that's simply not going to happen, though. It's not realistic. While some people claim that true productivity hovers at less than 1 hour per working day, you're going to calculate what you *think* yours is. Be honest. You may want to believe that you're productive for 8 out of the 10 hours, but if you go with that, you're only going to be hurting yourself if it's not true.

I suggest going with a quarter to a third. If you choose a third, then multiply that number by 3 and this will be your true value, what you need to charge per hour of work that you estimate a job will take.

Next, begin to attach a value to your time. Figure out how much a ten minute phone call will cost. Calculate how much a half hour meeting will cost. Determine how much that drive to the store for supplies will cost you. Then you'll begin to realize just how quickly time wasters take away from you on a daily basis. And then, hopefully, you'll be ready to eliminate as many as you can.

In truth, it's not possible to eliminate all of them, though. However, if you focus on getting rid of most of them, you'll be in a good position to maximize your earning potential.

Chapter 2 – Time Thieves

Don't you wish that there was something you could do when people try to steal something from you? Oh, right, there is. You call the police and report the theft. Sometimes the cops even find the thieves, arrest them, and then return your possessions. Sometimes they just find thieves and there's nothing to recover.

What about time thieves? What about those people who enjoy stealing our time make them want to come back again and again? Well, it's the fact that we *allow* them to.

We don't stand up to them or don't even recognize that they're stealing away our precious time. There are plenty of these people out there. You see them probably every day that you're breathing.

How about the person in line in front of you at the checkout for the supermarket? You know the one who's always talking to the cashier, slowing down the line, and making everyone behind her wait. Don't you just count the seconds until she finally, mercifully, gets her change, and her bags, and walks away?

Or how about the person who is constantly finding something to talk to you about? This person will generally lurk about near your office, waiting until you step outside, or tapping lightly on your door to ask you if you can spare a moment.

Maybe it's not one person; maybe it's an entire army of them, but one by one, those precious little minutes begin to add up. You are gracious because, frankly, you don't want to come across as being rude, so you smile even though inside you're ready to scream, and you hear them out, offer your two cents worth of advice, and try to escape. But, of course, most of the time they have more than one thing to say to you.

Then you have those people who seem to think that meetings are the best way to get things done. But since we just talked about productivity, how could sitting in meetings all day be a good way to get *anything* done? No one is actually being productive when they're in a meeting. All they're doing is talking. Talking about what they *need* to do, talking about what *should* get done, and no one's actually doing anything.

Along with those wonderful meetings is the relaxed atmosphere that so many people seem to have when it comes to them happening during the middle of the morning or afternoon. It seems that no one is in a big hurry to break from the meeting, so something that could have, or should have, taken 15 minutes suddenly lasts for another 15 or even 30 minutes. Talk about a waste of time!

You could probably find a host of time thieves surrounding you just about every day. You might not have thought about them in this light before, but now that you understand your time is the most valuable thing in the world to you and you won't ever get those minutes back once their stolen, you're going to begin noticing them everywhere.

You're the boss. You own this company that you're starting out, but that doesn't mean you should hire people to work for you who can't figure things out on their own, can't help each other when the need arises, or have to come to you for every little issue.

"Hey, boss, my computer keeps saying I need to restart, but when I do …"

"Do you know when we're supposed to get that shipment of supplies in?"

"Do you think …"

"Did you know …"

"I was thinking …"

They're everywhere. Do you honestly believe that your employee can't figure out that it's time to call a computer tech to have a look at that computer if it's having problems? Why do you need to know? If you're the only person who can determine these extra expenses, then you're opening yourself up to thieves. Time thieves.

What about some of the basics of your operation? Are you the only one who knows about shipments, orders, supply, stock, and so on? If so, then what are you thinking? Let it go! You won't be productive if you're spending all your time chasing after administrative things that you could be paying someone $15 per hour to tend to (quite a bit less than your hourly value, isn't it?)

How do you defeat time thieves?

The simple answer: you lock 'em up. You put them in jail.

Easier said than done, though, isn't it? Yes, it is, but it comes down to a simple choice, really. How much do you value your time? If you value it and you understand that productivity is where your earnings lie, then you have no choice, otherwise the time thieves will just continue to see you as the easy target and call on you to solve all their problems, or give them the excuse they're inherently looking for in order to be less productive (and of course, they are working for you so you're entire business is losing productivity).

First, you have to be firm in your office. You need to take charge. If you have five employees and each of them thinks that you're the person to chat to during the day, whether they're looking for a break or trying to buddy up with you, cut it off in the midst of their attempts.

"I'm sorry, but I'm busy right now. Catch me at the end of the day and we'll talk."

The end of the day. Once *all* of the work that you need to get done for that day is actually completed, then who cares if you waste a few minutes, right? But how many employees are going to stick around after they're done working to just chat with the boss?

Scheduling meetings for the end of the day is also a great idea. Do you think that people are going to want to prolong a meeting that starts 15 minutes before quitting time? No chance. They are going to want to get in, get the information they need, and get out so they can go home. No loitering around, no dragging the meeting out.

Can you imagine what other benefit there would be to a meeting schedule that takes place at the end of the day? Fewer meetings.

People are going to avoid scheduling them altogether. Most employees are protective of their quitting time. While some have no problem working late (whether they are hourly or salary employees), most just want to close up and go home. When they see another meeting scheduled for the end of the day, one of the first things they're going to do is call or text home to say they *might* be late, if the meeting runs late.

But that's not your goal; you're simply locking down your time from those thieves.

As for those pesky questions, set a simple rule: if it's not critical, drop a note in a suggestion type box. Tom ran out of pens and needs some more. The copier is running low on ink toner. The file cabinet isn't level, so it rattles when you open it. Whatever it is, you don't need to be bothered with it. Have a secretary or general employee tend to those things. You can have your assistant sift through the collection of notes at the end of the day and prioritize, so that if there is anything that you absolutely *must* address, you can do so then on the next day.

You defeat the time thieves when you take charge of your time, and your day. Most of us simply try to avoid confrontation, so we don't say anything, but that just gives them the opportunity to steal more time from you.

Remember, though, that most time thieves aren't consciously trying to steal your time. However, does it really matter if the thieves who stole your car weren't after yours but the one next to it? If you lost your ride, then no, it won't matter. It's still gone.

That's the way it is with your time; once it's gone, it's gone. It doesn't matter who stole it or why … you can't get it back and each minute that is stolen is time you can't ever recover.

Protect it from the time thieves by slapping handcuffs on them and tossing them in a cell. You can let them out from time to time if you want, but why would you want to? Your business is your livelihood, so protect it. Set you officers out to ensure that no thieves are lurking around you in the office.

Chapter 3 – Interruptions

Anyone who can state that they make it through their day without any interruptions is either naïve or a flat out liar. There's simply no way that you or anyone else can avoid interruptions, unless, of course, you unplug or turn off your phone and avoid going online.

As a business owner, interruptions are just a part of life. They surround us on a daily basis. You might not even realize that they're happening, but when enough of them build up, you're losing a lot of productive time during your day.

It's similar, in many respects, to the number of advertisements that the average person is exposed to on a daily basis. Would you believe me if I told you that we are exposed to about 2,000 ads per day? Sounds absolutely ridiculous, doesn't it? But what if I told you that those ads could be small ads you don't even notice? How about the billboards you pass on your way to work? Or the small signs in a store telling you about a great sale going on? Go to just about any major news site today and you'll see different ads all over them. Sure, you don't pay attention to them, but that doesn't mean they don't exist.

Now, out of those colossal number of ads, you might actually *notice* about 20 of them. Of that, you may remember three to four. So what do ads and interruptions have to do with each other?

Not much, except for the fact that even though you didn't notice most of those ads, it doesn't mean they don't exist. The same holds true for interruptions.

Just because you didn't notice something as being a distraction, cutting into your productivity, that doesn't mean that they didn't happen. You can think of them as ***interrproduc-***

Okay, so that's a made up word. So what? Make up your own if it helps you to remember that the enemy of productivity is interruptions. And just like that mountain of ads (and admit it now … you're looking around and starting to notice all of those thousands of ads, aren't you? Pretty amazing to finally realize what you're being subjected to on a constant and daily basis), they're everywhere.

The phone call.

The text message.

The quick question.

The inquiry from a client, or potential client.

The news item that just flashed across your screen.

The wife, or husband, or friend who needs you to pick up something on your way home from work.

The email.

The next email.

The mess of files and folders that you need to clean up once and for all.

Another email.

And the list goes on and on. And on. And on …

How can you recognize them? After all, you hadn't recognized them yet, so how are you going to be able to recognize them in the future?

That's a fairly easy answer. You'll recognize them when you determine your value (as we did in Chapter 1) and value your time.

You'll begin to be jealous of your time and when that happens, you're not going to want anything to get in the way of you doing the job that needs to be done.

In truth, recognizing interruptions is relatively easy, once you sit back and think about them in the right light. It's getting rid of them that tends to be the hard part. That's what we need to focus on now, though.

How to avoid interruptions

There are some things that are quite easy to do when it comes to getting rid of interruptions in our life. Some are a bit harder.

At Home

For those of you who are building your business from the comfort of your own home, you're going to face a whole litany of different temptations and possible interruptions. Most of them will be self-inflicted, such as taking a 'quick break' in the morning to go to the kitchen and grab a fresh cup of coffee, only to spend 20 minutes reading the newspaper before heading back to your office.

You could find yourself being surrounded by telemarketers calling the house phone, your spouse or kids making noise, asking questions, and acting as though your business is just a hobby and it's okay to interrupt you.

For that, you need to establish the rules. Set the expectations and make sure that everyone respects and adheres to them.

First, close your office door. Once the door is closed, no one should bother knocking or speaking through the door. For any reason. Not unless the house is on fire or there's another absolute emergency that must be tended to. Everyone in your family needs to respect the fact that this is your business and it's how you're going to make money for the family. If they can't respect that, then you may be best advised to find an office away from your home.

Kids shouldn't walk in or ask if they can go to a friend's house (interruption).

Your wife shouldn't tell you that the toilet's clogged again (interruption). What would she have done if you were at an office?

Your husband shouldn't ask you where the fabric softener is (interruption). He should already know that anyway.

Once the door is closed, that's it, no more talking to you –you've transcended to another plane. You'll return when the workday is over.

If you can't manage to cut yourself off from those interruptions, or you find that the distractions (such as TV, gaming systems, or anything else) are just too tempting, find an office space somewhere that you can easily afford. The bottom line is (the most important thing to concern yourself with) is productivity, so whatever you need to do in order to get that do

At the Office

If you are building a business away from the mountain of homemade distractions and interruptions, you still have a host of them to worry about.

You're the boss, the leader, the 'person with all the answers,' or so your employees like to believe (if you have any). Maybe you made them believe that they had to come to you before making any decisions.

Learn to let go and delegate (we'll get into that in more detail in Chapter 7). You can't do everything if you want to maximize productivity. The whole is greater than the sum of all its parts is a saying that holds true in this instance. It means your organization can do more and be more productive as a unit than all of your employees working independently. It means that you need to allow the rest of the organization to make decisions and answer their own questions.

It's one of the hardest things for an entrepreneur to do, though. Letting go of control feels like you're letting your business fly off on a random tangent. That's not the case, though. If you don't delegate, if you take on the burden of being the 'go to' person in your company for any and everything, then you're never going to get anything done. Everyone will be knocking on your door, calling your extension, or sending you an email asking you how to do this or that or whether they are allowed to do something. Forget it and step away from that role.

Make different people responsible for different decisions and aspects within the company.

If that doesn't work and you're constantly being bombarded still, then it may be time to get away from the office during the day. Turn your phone off and get your own work done. Within a few days, you'll be surprised to learn that most of your employees will have taken control and things are doing just fine without you.

If you don't give your team the confidence that they need to know that they can do this without you, then they're always going to be turning to you for answers and solutions. It's time to step away from that slippery slope.

What about phone calls? It's tough to know who's calling you all of the time, especially if you get inquiries from potential clients. You don't really want those clients to go somewhere else, but you need to get some projects done, right?

Establish certain times during the day where you'll be available for phone calls. This could be 9am to 10pm and again at 5pm to 6pm. You can take the messages that you received and return the calls or take incoming calls. Have one of your employees (if it's not a receptionist or assistant) answer all calls coming in for you. He or she should take a message and let them know that you will return his or her call within that specified timeframe. If that doesn't work for them, your receptionist should find out when is best to reach them and arrange it with them. Most people are flexible when it comes to a phone call. You may even discover that many of the calls you field are related to basic questions that other employees could easily answer.

What about the cell phones? When you have a cell phone, you are essentially 'in touch' all of the time. This is where you simply need to make a decision: do you want to take charge of your life and your *productivity* or do you want to be a slave to a mobile device?

If you think you're really that important that you can't leave home without it, then you have other problems to worry about other than trying to find ways to make more money. No one can help you with that, and what you do in your personal time is your business, but when you're at work, shut the cell phone off, stuff it in a drawer, and don't think about it until quitting time. It's really quite simple, actually. Try it someday … it may just be the best thing you ever do.

Email. Boy, if there was ever a worse creation, it would have to be email. Sure, it's made getting in touch with people easier, but it seems that some people think every thought and idea they ever had should be sent by this form of communication.

Set up at least two email accounts for you at your business. One for the very important things, such as emails from your personal assistant and top level clients and one for everything else. Let everyone in your office know that you only check the 'everything else' email once a week, usually on a Monday, though you could certainly do it on Friday. Mid-week isn't a good idea because you could get trapped in a list of interruptions all over again.

Check your important email account daily, once when you arrive at work and once when you're getting ready to leave. Set aside 15 minutes each time to answer them. This can usually be done when you're going through phone messages.

Lastly, when you are planning on taking or making phone calls, set up an exit strategy.

"Hi, (so and so), I'm happy to speak with you, but I have to let you know that I'll be heading out in 5 minutes, so we need to make this quick."

It's simple, somewhat crude, but it gets the point across. Don't be sorry for such a short call; be direct. Your time is *valuable* to you and you're going to guard it ruthlessly if needed.

Never apologize for being successful. That will only tear down what you're working so hard to build.

Now that we know the different kinds of distractions that abound, and how to cut them off at the knees, it's time to dig into that other productivity killer:

Procrastination.

Chapter 4 – Procrastination

Why do today what you can put off until tomorrow.

This is a common, somewhat humorous phrase that highlights the procrastinator's motto.

There's a cartoon out there that pictures a slovenly man, hands in pockets, arriving at a door with a sign on the glass that reads: Procrastinators Anonymous. On a handwritten note below, a note reads: Tonight's meeting postponed. To be rescheduled eventually.

Procrastination is a serious problem for millions of business men and women around the world. It's the concept of delaying doing something for whatever reason. Even though you know that you can and *should* do something today, you delay it for an hour or a day or a week.

What's the big deal with procrastination, though? After all, when you have to do something, and eventually do it, what's the big deal? It got done, right?

Usually when people procrastinate, they do it by busying themselves with something else, some other distraction. When you get involved with distractions, what does that lead to? A loss of productivity.

To explain this a bit further, think about the last thing that you didn't *want* to do, even though you knew at some point you'd *have* to get it done. It could have been a visit with the in-laws or taking out the garbage or having a meeting with a person that you'd known for a long time, but who you had to terminate from your employment.

There are plenty of things that we need to get done even though we don't want to do them. So what was yours? What was the last thing that you procrastinated doing, for whatever reason?

Now, what did you do to *avoid* doing it? You had to make some kind of excuse for not getting it done. At least, most of us need an excuse, otherwise we feel *guilty*. So what was the excuse? What did you end up doing instead of what you needed to get done?

When it comes to work, when we procrastinate on a project, we tend to do something that isn't productive. We might look through those emails or listen to voicemail messages, even though we know we should be doing that other thing as soon as possible.

You see, when you procrastinate, you're not just delaying something that you need to get done, but you're cutting down on your productivity. It's a sad cycle that leads to a significant loss of productivity.

How can you avoid procrastinating?

One of the best ways to stop procrastinating is writing down in a journal every day what you *need* to get done that day. You might have a major project that will take you 40 hours to complete, but on this day, you may want to (or plan to) devote 5 solid hours to working on it.

If you have trouble committing to working on a project like that, then you should focus on breaking that down into smaller increments. Write down that you'll work on that project between 10am and 11am, no matter what. Right at 10am, you're going to stop whatever you're doing and start working on that major project.

Dive right in and don't allow yourself to think about it because if you start thinking about it, you might put it off. After all, it's not due for two weeks, right? So what's the big deal if you don't get those five hours done today?

The big deal is that if you put it off until tomorrow, what are you going to be doing today that will be productive?

Writing tasks down on a daily basis, broken down by the hour, can be a great way to get more done in your day. Breaking projects – no matter what size- down into the smallest increments possible will help you stick to your schedule. For example, if you broke that five hour block you set aside to work on that project tomorrow into five separate hours, you can reward yourself with something you enjoy, like a five minute web surf of all those news sites you enjoy scrawling through. Those five minutes will eat away at your productivity, but in the beginning, they can help procrastinators by offering valuable rewards.

If you still have trouble, have someone else hold you accountable. When you do that, when someone is checking on your progress, it can be a powerful motivator.

Chapter 5 - Time Management

Do you manage your time well? Do you have a fairly good idea about how long you spend working on something or how much time you devote to those pesky things we call administrative functions? If you don't, then it's time that you did. After all, every single one of those 'things' that don't actually earn you money (those things that you can't call 'billable' hours) are things that don't have a high priority. For anyone.

So how is your time management?

Do you tend to just 'wing it' and get through your day? Do you write down a list of tasks that you need to complete, but not how long you expect each to take or how long you're willing to spend working on them? If you don't estimate how long something will take you, then how could you possible manage your time well throughout the day?

How long does it take you to read a memo that is a page long? How long does it take you to sift through 100 email messages? How about phone calls? Do you know how long you tend to spend talking to someone else on the phone, whether it's a client, spouse, or friend?

Most of us, until we are pressed on the issue, have no clue just how much time we (waste) spend doing all of those little tasks that we have throughout the day.

Right now, without thinking about it too much (in other words, try to be honest with yourself), jot down how much time you spend doing all of the extraneous tasks that aren't considered billable hours throughout your day. Try not to cut a call short or flip through your messages faster than you normally do just because you think this is a test. Instead, when you're honest with yourself about this, you'll be able to see the patterns that arise.

You will most likely notice that you spend a great deal more time on these non-necessity tasks than you initially thought. In fact, when you consider that some people are only productive for less than an hour out of an eight-hour day, you can begin to understand why that is.

We spend too much time on frivolous stuff and that's time that you're never going to be able to get back or earn back.

When you begin to track your daily tasks and how much time you spend doing 'nothing' (nothing being a term that refers to non-billable, unproductive time), you realize quickly how much time you waste and why you need to begin tracking it and managing your time much more efficiently.

When I say 'unproductive' time, that doesn't mean that you're being completely unproductive; you could be bidding on new jobs, talking to prospects, and answering questions that could lead to more jobs in the future. That's great and leads you to more work, but it's not actually earning you any money.

So, with that being said, do you think that you could have cut the phone or Skype interview that lasted 48 minutes down, especially for a job that isn't going to cover your hourly rate? Yes. You could have cut off the conversation after 5 minutes. If they're not willing to pay what your *value* is, then why bother staying on the line?

But what if they end up having a ton of other work to give me later?

If that's the case, then you'll be chasing every single potential client around who claims to have a lot of work waiting to get done. If they value your experience and knowledge, they'll pay. If not, they won't. Forget about a 'trial period' or other nonsense like that; your portfolio speaks to your skills and qualifications. Have some self respect enough to say, "I'm busy with projects today, but if you are impressed with my portfolio and have a couple of quick questions, I'm more than happy to answer them. *But I have a meeting in five minutes.*"

They might be offended, they might be surprised, but they can't give you the time back that you end up wasting trying to convince them to hire you when *it doesn't even meet your value*.

When you begin to keep track of your time and how long you spend on different tasks, even the distractions that you may need from time to time to help clear your mind to allow those powerful creative juices to flow, you'll begin to see just how much time during your day you're being 'productive.'

Does it surprise you? Did you believe that you were actually *more* productive than that? If so, then it's time to see how you could improve your 'system.'

By improving your time management system, you need to first accept that you're not being as efficient and effective as you would like.

Then you need to be willing to do what it takes to become more productive. This could mean leaving your cell phone in your car, shutting off or blocking access to your favorite guilty pleasure websites, or whatever it is that distracts you.

Use some of the advice I've already outline in this book, such as limit your email or phone time during the day. Schedule any necessary meetings for the end of the day. Close your door and let everyone know that when it's closed, don't knock and don't bother.

Use a calendar and keep track of *everything* that you *need* to do and whether you actually get it done. You might be surprised by how quickly you can change your time management skills, all because you begin monitoring it all.

Chapter 6 – Information Overload

I still remember when the Internet was this new toy that a few people began playing with. It was cute, funny, and offered us a chance to get in touch with people we hadn't seen in a long time. Back in the 1990s when the main way to connect was through that notorious dial tone and robotic argument, few people really could foresee just how powerful it would become.

Today, we're inundated with information. Just about anything you want to learn about, find, or buy can be located on the Internet. Back in the 1990s, we were already being overloaded with information, so now it's a hundred times more severe and there doesn't seem to be any end in sight. In fact, the more technology advances, the more information we have access to.

Whether you visit the bookstore, go to your local public library, or go online, you're going to be met with books, newspapers, magazines, blogs, commentary, social media, and on and on and on. Where does it end?

How can you sift through the massive amount of information out there?

In order to be successful in anything that you do in life, you need to have the right information at your disposal. More and more items are being published, either in print form or online, every single year. Most of it is drivel and doggerel (poorly written garbage) that offers no real value, even if it's in line with what you're trying to research.

So how can you get through the information overload?

First, determine the source.

People love Wikipedia, but it's an open source network, which means that it's not always reliable and can be altered to provide false or misleading information. Imagine you needed to back up a report for a client with facts and you reference a Wikipedia page, only to find out three weeks later that all of that information was false. Not only does your client look bad for what you gave him, but you could be in trouble if he decides to file a lawsuit against you.

Certain sources have specific biases and leanings. Some are more reliable than others. Seek out professionally accepted and respected publications and focus on them.

Next, specialize. You may have a great deal of knowledge and expertise in writing, but if you try and take on every type of project, you're going to become overwhelmed just trying to figure it all out. Specialize in fiction, or non-fiction for example. Business plans may be your strength. Or perhaps it's copy. Whatever it is, focus on that niche when looking for information on it. This will save you a great deal of time by avoiding all of the information about those other niches.

Learn to read faster and more effectively. When we're taught to read, we're taught to read out loud. The teacher wanted to make sure that we pronounced the words we were learning properly, but what do you tend to do now? If you're like most people, you probably read 'aloud' inside your head. There's that voice in your head that is reading each word. The problem is that this limits most people to a reading rate of about 120 to 160 words per minute, at the most.

It would take you about 11 hours to get through a short book. That's a long time when you consider that your *time is valuable*.

Learn to speed read. There are courses that you can take that will help you increase your reading rate to 500, 600, or even several thousands of words per minute. The faster you read, the faster you'll get through plenty of information.

You could have someone sift through your usual haunts to pick out the most pertinent and relevant information for you. This could be a secretary or even someone who is looking to make a few extra dollars at home. You tell him or her what you want and they send you the information. They'll go through the latest mountain of info and send you *only* what you would want to read. If they prove worthy and effective, keep them on. If not, cut them loose and try someone else.

Get into audio books. If you drive a lot, there's a lot of time that you could be spending getting more information into your system. Every mile could be one more tidbit of useful information that would save you from having to read about it when your time is of the essence.

Stop watching TV shows. Okay, this might be tough for some people, but if you value your time, then it's time to cut free of the colorful brain drain. If you absolutely *must* watch a certain program, record it on DVR. Skip the commercials and that hour long program suddenly only takes 40 minutes!

Cut free of the useless news and information. Sure, there are some important things that go on in the news, but let's face it: you don't need to read about 200 different editorials or news articles about Obamacare, or the latest professional athlete going to jail or the latest celebrity divorce. What good does any of that do for you?

Answer: nothing. Nada. Forget about it (or, as a Brooklyn New Yorker might say, Fugheddaboudit).

Technology offers many distractions, but it can also provide some useful tools. You might actually discover that you can get tidbits of information, about the length of a Tweet (Twitter, if you don't know yet), and be able to determine whether it might be of interest to you. Still, you need to monitor yourself to make sure that none of that is actually a distraction.

You want to make sure that you focus on *only the information that will benefit you directly*. Specialize, in other words. Anything else beyond that is wasted time and you aren't up for that anymore, are you? After all, you now truly

Value your time!

Chapter 7 – Delegate

You know everything about your business, don't you? Sure you do. Just like almost every other business owner in the past, you probably have done just about everything there is to do in your company.

However, can you do them better than everyone else? That may be up for debate. Not to insult you, but when you hire people to work for you, you're looking for the best of the best, right? Unless you own a fast food restaurant and are only able to offer minimum wage, you're going to have some pretty good employees working for you.

It's time to accept the fact that when you try to do things (tasks) that others in your organization are fully capable of doing, especially people who make less than you, then you're paying yourself too much to do the work that someone else could do for less. It doesn't make much business sense.

That's why you need to learn to delegate responsibilities and assignments to other people.

It may be the toughest thing for the owner of a business to do, but it's also one of the most important. When you build your business from the ground up, you want to make sure that it stays on the upward trajectory that you set for it. What happens if you begin to delegate out certain responsibilities and it all falls apart?

Well, if that were to happen –which is not likely, if you hired the right people to work for you- then those mistakes won't likely be all that costly and you'd be able to get back on track quickly enough. You're not handing the keys to your brand new beach house to a 17 year old popular high school kid, after all.

Accept the fact that you don't have all the answers, nor should you *try* to have all the answers. You may know just about everything about your business, but the way you do things may not be the most efficient or effective. By delegating out certain tasks to qualified people, you could end up discovering more efficient ways of doing things.

Sometimes, too, if the job is getting done, even if it's not the way you would like it to be done, and even if it's not great, it just might be good enough. If it doesn't negatively impact your business, then so what? If you want your stock room to look a certain way, but the employee you assigned to manage it arranged everything differently, so what? If it works and it's effective and efficient, so what? Let go.

In order to delegate out tasks effectively and efficiently, you need to define the task. Let the person know what they need to do. Ask them questions to ensure that he or she knows what has to get done. Show them how you would like it to be done (but this doesn't mean that's how it will ultimately be done, especially if they find a more efficient way of doing it). Establish a deadline or check-in time to make sure that they are doing it properly. Finally, make sure that your employee fully understands all of those expectations and parameters.

Now, you need to fire someone. That someone is you. Any task of job that you take on that can be performed by someone making a lot less than you should be delegated.

Sit back and write down all of the things that you do that fall into this category and simply fire yourself. There, that wasn't so bad, was it?

Now get on to more important, more *productive* things, will you?

Chapter 8 – People Who Are Full of Shit

Well, there it is. People who are full of shit.

We're surrounded by them. Didn't you know that? So many people seem to know an awful lot about everything. And they want *you* to know it. Or at least they want you to believe what they say. That doesn't make them right. So who are these people who are constantly surrounding us and who are so full of shit?

They're the people that 'know everything.' They're the ones who want to tell you how you *should* be running your business, who tell you what mistakes you're making, and who might be talking behind your back to your employees and everyone else around you that they would do it better, they know better, and that you're going to run your business into the ground.

Hey, it's easy to play poker when it's not your money. When you're gambling with other people's money, are you going to take chances? Sure. Why not? After all, it didn't cost you anything to get that money.

What happens when it's *your* money on the line? You tend to be much more careful, you tend to think through your decisions better, and you don't gamble. You may make decisions that could be considered a bit of a gamble at times, but you do so based on educated assumptions. After all, starting a business is, in reality, a gamble. You're putting your money and –and more importantly- your *time* on the line when you start a business, and there are no guarantees.

When you do, you'll suddenly be surrounded by people who know everything about what you should do.

"Why did you hire that person?"

"You should be focused on such-and-such if you want to …"

"If it were my business, I would …"

And the list would go on and on. You can't avoid them because they will *always* find a way to infiltrate your life and your business. But what do they want?

People who are full of shit want attention. They want the spotlight that they didn't earn. They want to gain some recognition. Why? It could be that they're insecure and want to feel as though *someone* thinks they're better than they are. It could be that they want everyone else to believe that they can handle more responsibility. Or they simply don't want to see you successful, and if you end up being successful, they can try and claim some responsibility for that.

They're full of shit because in reality they *don't* know, they *don't* have the answers that you would want or need, and they *don't* have the guts to put their own money and time on the line for anything. They'd rather sit in the shadows where it's safe.

Some people might call them Armchair quarterbacks. These are the people who probably never played any sport after high school but seem to know exactly what every professional athlete did wrong on every play. They're the 'I could have made that play' person who can't even get up off the couch. Or want to.

So how do you avoid them? How do you deal with people who are full of shit?

First, recognize them for who they are. Sometimes they may be hard to spot. They may *sound* like they know what they're talking about, but if you are being lulled into the confidence of someone who might know something that you don't, research it. Find out for sure.

Next, once you know who these people are, if they work for you, invite them into your office (at the end of the day) and explain to them what their job is here, what their responsibilities are, and tell them that if they can't handle that, then they won't have a place within your organization any longer.

If the person who is full of shit is a friend, you can kindly ask them to avoid discussing your business with you. If they can't abide by that, then limit your contact or your conversations with that person.

If the individual is family, then you can sit down with them and anyone else in your family and kindly request that they support you, but that you've done plenty of work and don't want to mix your business with your relationships.

The other way to avoid people who are full of shit is to stop answering your phone when they call, stop opening up the welcome mat for them and if they ask you why you've done that, then you can tell them. Honestly, you don't need it. Not now. Not again.

All they're doing is taking up your *valuable time*. Now that you know what's truly valuable, you have to simply take charge and tune them out. You have the means and the technology. You just need to step up and do it.

Do you have the desire? Does it matter?

Of course.

Conclusion

Time is the most precious and valuable thing that you have. When you treat it with the proper respect, when you understand how to manage your time, avoid distractions, cut out interruptions, and put those people who are full of shit in their place, you'll be able to get more done, be more productive, and make more money.

You won't be able to get those lost minutes back in your life. Make them count.

Every single one of them.

Money talks every day and it says the same thing over and over …

Value your time and the rest will fall into place.

If you need further assistance I offer one on one coaching through my Entrepreneur Mentorship Program. For more information and a Free Consultation just visit:

http://www.makeprofitseasy.com

Good luck and I wish you much success with your entrepreneurial endeavors.

Sincerely,

Omar Johnson

Other Books Available By Author On Kindle, Audio and Paperback

How To Transform Yourself From Employee To Online Entrepreneur: Escaping The 9 To 5 Wage Slave Syndrome

The Killer Instinct: How To Master It and Achieve Anything That You Want

Winning Habits: Getting Rid of A Loser's Mentality

Conquering Your Fears

Passive Income: Stop Working Hard For Your Money And Let Your Money Work Hard For You

How To Create A Profitable Ezine From Scratch

The Secrets Of Making $10,000 on Ebay in 30 Days

The Complete Guide To Investing in Gold And Silver: Surviving The Great Economic Depression

How To Sell Any Product Online:"Secrets of The Killer Sales Letter"

Smart Money: How To Get Out Of The Consumer Trap And Invest Your Money Wisely

How To Make A Fortune Using The Public Domain

Search Engine Domination: The Ultimate Secrets To Increasing Your Website's Visibility And Making A Ton Of Cash

Creative Real Estate Investing Strategies And Tips

How to Make Money Online:"The Savvy Entrepreneur's Guide To Financial Freedom"

How to Overcome Your Self-Limiting Beliefs & Achieve Anything You Want

The Secrets of Finding The Perfect Ghostwriter For Your Book

The Creative Real Estate Marketing Equation: Motivated Sellers + Motivated Buyers = $

How To Start An Online Business With Less Than $200

How To Market Your Business Online and Offline

Money Blueprint: The Secrets To Creating Instant Wealth

Affiliate Cash: How To Make Money As An Affiliate Marketer

How To Promote Market And Sell Your Kindle Book

AudioBook Profits: How To Make Money by Turning Your Kindle, Paperback and Hardcover Book into Audio.

The Fine Art of Writing The Next Best Seller on Kindle

Fast Cash: 9 Amazing Ways To Make Money Without Having To Work At A Job

Money Magnet: How to use the Laws of the Universe to Attract Money into Your Life

Hypnotic Influence: How To Create A Cult Like Following For Anything That You Do

The Art of Manipulation: How to Get Anybody to Do What You Want

Jobless Cash: How to Make Money if You're Unemployed or Just Plain Tired of Working for Someone Else

What They Didn't Teach You In School About Money

www.ingramcontent.com/pod-product-compliance
Lightning Source LLC
Chambersburg PA
CBHW071805170526
45167CB00003B/1185